THE PLAYGROUND BELL

Adam Johnson

THE PLAYGROUND BELL

CARCANET

First published in 1994 by
Carcanet Press Limited
208-212 Corn Exchange Buildings
Manchester M4 3BQ

A CIP catalogue record for this book
is available from the British Library
ISBN 1 85754 064 6

The publisher acknowledges financial assistance
from the Arts Council of Great Britain

Set in 10 pt Joanna by Bryan Williamson, Frome
Printed and bound in England by SRP Ltd, Exeter

Note

Three weeks before his death in May 1993 at the age of twenty-eight, Adam Johnson delivered the substantially complete draft version of this book to Carcanet; at that time, a separate and somewhat smaller collection, *The Spiral Staircase*, which was published by Acumen in July 1993, had already gone to press.

My aim in preparing *The Playground Bell* for publication has been to present as nearly as possible the book which Adam would have wanted. Editorial intervention has therefore been absolutely minimal and restricted to two simple matters. Firstly, though the arrangement of the text is not strictly chronological (there are, for instance, a couple of quite late poems at the beginning), it does have an overall drift, deepening and darkening as it progresses towards the very fine pieces he wrote in his last year or so. Bearing this in mind, it seemed right to move one poem, 'The Break' (which dates from July 1991), from the relatively untroubled early pages to its more appropriate chronological and thematic place in the centre of the book; at the suggestion of Adam's mother, Joyce Johnson, 'The Playground Bell', written in December 1992, appears at the end of the book.

Secondly, although Adam's text was virtually book-length – presented with an elegance and accuracy designed to put copy-editors out of business – it was nevertheless a draft to which he would certainly have added further material if he had lived: 'I think I can write another fifteen or so,' he said in his covering letter to Michael Schmidt. From 1985 until his death, he showed or sent me copies of all his poems, and I have therefore been able to add a handful which do not appear in *The Spiral Staircase*: '26 June 1986', 'The Fire', 'Poem for the Nineteenth of October', 'Brumal' and 'Heavy my Gold-Ball-Baby'. There are at least another two dozen early poems, including those which appeared in his first pamphlet *In the Garden* (1986), which I'm certain he would not have considered as contenders for this collection, as well as several shorter pieces written as birthday or Christmas cards: it may eventually be possible to collect these with Adam's complete poems in a single volume, but that will be a different sort of a book and a different sort of occasion.

NEIL POWELL

for Staiszu James Lovendoski

Acknowledgements

Some of the poems in this collection have previously appeared in the following magazines and journals: *The European Gay Review, Interim, Outposts, PEN International, PN Review, Prospice, The Rialto,* and in a pamphlet published by *The Hearing Eye Press.*

Contents

Nocturne

October makes censers
Of these wooded places.
Out of the cool ether
Of darkness strike the
Branching crystals of trees,
By night's definition
Of a rarer substance –
The texture of bark
Is wholly light's privilege.

The path leads us to
A locked gate we climb. There is
Tension in our nearness –
The feel of you, our hands
Clasped in recognition
Of their own engaged warmth.

In embracing we earth,
Here, where a stream's course
Through banks of cypresses
Designs a garden,
The motion of its cool blade
As purposeful as blood.

Now the spell of your voice
Concedes to other sound,
Falling into dark air
That cherishes each note –
This water easing
Over known rocks, through reeds,
The soft consent of leaves.
Drawing me close, there is
Nothing you would not give.

SW5

Pigeons are mating on a window-sill
Above the traffic in the Earl's Court Road.
We dare not risk such informality,
But have a way of looking and a code:
   Owning no feathers,
   We sport our leathers.

Bluebottle

Little motorised bead, you are
A beast of remarkable stupidity –
Insisting as you do on that
Illegible aerial scrawl. How can this,
A very navigable space,
Confound even so unreasoning a brain?

Too late! I am bored with this game.
You ricochet, land at last on the curtain.
Under my aimed swipe, you split in its fabric,
A small coal, a cooling fragment.

Chaotic, iridescent thing,
Looking at your smashed body I remember
Our existence is relative.

26 June 1986

It is summer, and here, upon a bench
which lazes on the rise of this
city park, I sit, unspecial in
the easy scene.

Nearby, a boy reclines, shirtless in
the shadow-fingering of leaves.
He is writing, as I am writing;
and suddenly, the intimacy
of this moment brings to me
an image of our unity –
though we shall never touch,
and he will never know my name.

The Night Ferry

for Colin Hunter

Wherever we must home to (even via
    the port of Dover where the English
perfected the art of delay) it is worth noting
    that going back accounts for
less time at sea than does an outward voyage –
    or seemingly:
              Perhaps
a sense of the inevitable – work,
    the post, the awful news –
merely restores to us the familiar topography
    of the place we keep our days in,
where even strangers talk in our own language –
    though rarely after dawn
in a public bar.
              (On the Warmoesstraat,
    in a quarter of the city
whose every portal is hospitable,
    we have discussed the universe
with gods who drink jenever with their breakfast).
    Whether our peregrinations
are solitary or made with one we trust
    will keep us from being bored
between lunch and dinner, a last evening encroaches.
    And now, a mile or so
off shore, alone, still fairly drunk, I stand,
    look back across the stern
to where Zeebrugge is a slick of lights
    anonymous among
the coded stars, and think of every face,
    awed by the same night,
whose mouth 'O's with the names of continents –
    Boredom and Loneliness.
Freedom in transit, then – at a given instant
    not to be anywhere?

But this unhomely vessel is no time machine –
     land, though not in sight,
lies dead ahead.
                  We'll turn our watches back,
     glad if we have been missed,
and go together down St Martin's Lane.

The Fire

for Neil Powell

And yes, we grow ironic as we learn:
Bland hope, lit by the truth, condemns the fool –
Whose fear of reason bids him pass the time
With fools – who, as all men, must die alone.
His word is branded with an insane fire:
Keep faith without conviction – ethics lie.

Trust in the senses, or condone the lie –
Religions, like policemen, never learn.
The road to freedom leaves a trail of fire,
Which all must follow blindly with the fool.
And he that travels, travels best alone,
In owing nothing but his place in time.

And yes, we have the best of worlds. In time
Each gift assumes the pattern of a lie –
Man cannot live by happiness alone,
The mirror shows us more than we would learn:
The patriot will recognise the fool,
Naked with him in liberty and fire.

The poet's hand commands a living fire
That feeds the burning currency of time:
Exactitude and form dissolve the lie
That politicians weave. For every fool
A government exists. The more we learn,
We learn to keep the flame that burns alone.

A star flares to the touch. Not love alone
But loyalty is tested in its fire.
We reach and reach for what we cannot learn
As critics come and go. Great in their time,
True to their trade, forgive them when they lie –
Only the just have leave to judge the fool.

Deep in the eye of man, perceive a fool
Whose vision is unique. In him alone
Does fear of death give credence to the lie
That to his end salvation bends its fire.
Hope marks his grave – the shoveller is time:
Interred therein, all he will ever learn.

And yet, the swiftest envoy is the fool,
Who walks the darkened watershed alone:
His words are dressed with roses, but they lie.

The Gift

for Don Bachardy
on The Last Drawings of Christopher Isherwood

In work that loved the eye was merciless –
Catching its subject in that act of death –
But read consent between the lines of pain
And from decay construed its otherness:

Here is the black word drawn under the breath –
Painted to light, veracious and humane –
Motive and consummation in our art
Who live uncertain of its certain terms.

Should our chief dread incite us to reprove
The draughtsman for his honesty, we start
To counter all that artifact affirms –
For not to censor is an act of love.

Table Manners

for Paul Gambaccini

I had forgotten that: the way
Your right hand sometimes holds your fork
(The wrong hand those who know would say),
Idly suspended as you talk –

The way I always have. A pen
I similarly use. As light
Procures the page it shows again
Not how we speak but how we write.

The love of friends – from every school –
Defines us, not by etiquette,
But by a law more durable,
Made, not in heaven, or, not yet.

April Shower

The April rain irradiates the street,
Beading the curtained sunlight at the door.
No-one I know walks in. A song begins.
I can't think why I come here any more.

The surly kid who's managing the bar,
Fondles a ring of keys: he used to be
The glass-collector here. Promoted since,
He checks the progress of a camp trainee

Whose looks are perfect, though he cannot pull
His pints and won't survive a week of this.
One of the old boys waves a twenty note
And orders gin and tonic with a kiss.

He's got his eye on something for the evening –
This bleachy kitten sporting mucky pumps –
And wonders how to get him back to Bromley.
The laser in the cd-player jumps.

It's time to go. My glass brims with the glare
From the wet pavement. I never liked this tune.
The barboy lisps we'll see you later. Maybe.
If he's still here tomorrow afternoon.

Station Buffet, Ipswich

In light grey jeans shorn off above the knee,
With cotton sleeves rolled up, strong boots cross-laced,
He's dressed for some adventure out of doors.

His girl companions watch me watching him –
Bizarre collusion in desire's exchange
He's too engrossed in reading to observe.

His focus alters as he turns a page,
Courting distraction with an upward glance
That takes in half the room. Instinctively

I shift my gaze onto the farther wall,
Steady my thought-train on its ringing lines,
And catch him waving in a bright cartoon.

Poem for the Nineteenth of October

for my mother

After September's embers lazing
    Weld the stamens in the rose,
And leaves that twist and hang amazing
    Grow profound in their repose;
As equinoctial brilliance renders
    Every form in deeps and golds,
A sybaritic Venus tenders
    Gifts of love October holds:
With arabesques in halls of air,
    This naked daughter of the sky
Be partnered with you everywhere,
    Who dances for she cannot die.

The Dancing Partner

Forty odd years ago you nearly died,
When, as you turned, a bullet brushed your teeth
Leaving behind a taste like nicotine.
In retrospect a shocking accident,
Though, seconds later, you were still alert –
The foliage was thorned with bayonets,
The trees fruited with eyes.
                                    Burma it was,
Far out of Lancashire and even wetter –
The Monsoon dark that glutted in the bone,
The trenches deep with maggots, pencil snakes –
Knowing, one afternoon, the sudden chill,
The sure prognostic of malaria.
After six months, eight out of forty men
Survived to shake the leeches from their boots
And sailed for England, late-comers at the party.

And after it all the continuum of death,
And the endless pointless hanging on, the waste
Of blood and talent in defence of borders –
For heaven is a dry place with no trees,
Or a place of water, densely forested,
With good roads that traverse no hostile quarter –
But not here, and not now.
                                    Stay drunk if you can –
Sleep in your bamboo body till the day.
Sunset and starset, countless numbers fall.

The Colour of Trees

in memoriam Eardley Knollys, 1902-1991

Behind the blue corolla of your eye,
You wandered in a landscape where the trees
Grew in amazement at your love of them –
Plausibly red, or bronzy where they fell
In a Hampshire wood.
                High on the fields of Spain,
Alone in the Serrania de Ronda,
You walked for hours in cerulean valleys,
Observed the reinventions of the light
On house-tops, followed the *camino* back,
Through sheer perspective, down the vivid chases
Toward a gallery off West Halkin Street
You hung with branches from al-Ahmar's garden.

The Reunion

In my last nightmare, Gary Jones,
The faceless councillors had built
One vast estate across the Northern hills –
A labyrinth of unadopted streets
Without provision for a single wood,
Where playgrounds lay unmarked, four acres square,
That had been reservoirs,
Their walls inclined and set with broken glass.

In my last nightmare, Gary Jones,
You were the gentle reaver at my side –
Through rain-dark red-brick terraces,
My vandal brother.
We were young-old as the gangs
Pursued us, shouting, but afraid of you –
My father's name
Loud in their teeth, their hands
All red around the stones that weighed their pockets.
– Young-old and strangers when we reached
A quarry's edge, flung backwards by the wind:
'This is the place,' you said. 'You will be safe
Among these rocks.'
      On our last day at school,
When you ran past me through the wire-mesh gate –
Friend, at the last, of all my enemies –
I wept all down the long hill back
By unknown ways,
And could not recognise my mother's house.

Green Fingers

I cleave from the live stem
Its leaf – a pearled ellipse,
Divided by the darker midrib. Here,
A tap-root will emerge,
Through water in a glass.
I love its bright potentiality –
The pattern of these veins.
A miracle
Charges the nucleus.

But look how the green world
Lies burning at the feet of men.

High Force

Light's elver-fury of terrible water,
A hawser-thrash across these Pennine shoulders –
Through Caldron Snout, under the Cronkley Scar,
And rocks that brace against its wild kinetics –
Past high ground where the Celtic hunter-farmers
Had laboured in their windy settlements,
And down the bastions of shale and whinstone
Into a flight of whips.
                            Growing in thunder,
The juniper and mealy primula –
And at the watershed blue gentians
Still prove the radiance of a timid fuse.

Spring Poem

for Jeremy Trafford

If you are by nature green,
enjoying a tendency
to bear foliage, you may
now be well pleased with yourself.

Narcissus poeticus,
local even in cities,
be especially joyful.
Even a determined grouch –
one for whom piles of dead leaves
are the ultimate turn-on –
acknowledges your being
with a twinge of gratitude.

Dominant in our woodlands,
Endymion nonscriptus,
perennial harbinger
of a temperate future
and long walks in important
silence, you may consider
your come-back a sensation.

Forsythia, what can I say…

Human, let us try to be
comparably generous
with our natural talents,
being as vulnerable,
and equally disinclined
to turn away from the sun.

Brumal

This cold weather
Renders other
That lights farther:
Perceive beyond

The rimed fences
Sunlight lances –
That bright dance is
A sea of land.

A quinquereme
Laden with brume
Trawls in the loam,
Makes aqueous

The nearest field:
Standing, a child,
Drowned in his world,
Oblivious.

Poem

And I am also this water
           and this rock,
And these furled leaves, that twist out
           and become my hands.
I am the root of the first tree,
           and a new forest:
The soil runs in my veins, seeking
           its own river.
Walking through rain I can touch you,
           for you wet my skin,
And we fall into step as you cross a street
           in another city,
Or turn at the door of your own house,
           where I also live.

Safe Sex

We meet in the interstices of dreams –
Behind the bike sheds north of Erebus –
In back rooms and dark alleys of the mind.

I hold to every pulse – his, his, my own –
Stare through his eye and endlessly appraise
The metamorphoses of a nameless god.

Our nights are epic, vanished in a turn
That pulls me out of sleep, awed like a child
Claiming his hero with the first embrace.

The Break

Night-sweat –
                    the cold shock –
A door blown out,
Banging across the deck
Of the nightmare boat
Where I run, seasick,
Out of the rolling bar
Into incredible rain,
Fall through the black air –
And half wake, shivering,
As I hit the sea.
                    My tongue
Cuts on a silent shout,
With a dry side-trick
That works my levered eye.

The room. Half-light
Barely delineates
A chair – transmogrifies
The pattern that repeats
Ingenious plumes along
The height of the far wall
To grotesque hieroglyph –
Weird totems that conceal
Some runic epitaph.

I clench, unclench my mind.
All senses charge, engage
The neural machinery
Of limbs, fingers, a hand:
My pulse tingles.
                    I see
The curtain taking edge,
Through gradations of blond
To substantivity.

The dream breaks on the day.
Guessing it's five a.m.
Or so, I hear outside
The plangent interplay
Between traffic and bird,
And recognise the same
Dull panic and dismay.

I lift the single sheet.
What is the world doing?
And what does this light mean?
In case some miracle
Is working in the street,
I rush to the window, lean
Right out over the sill.
Nothing to report.
It must have rained. That's all.
Just colder than I thought.

Heavy my Gold-Ball-Baby

for my hamster

Heavy my gold-ball-baby,
The swing of my waking –
Night had me rocked under,
Safe in his oubliette.

Blood-thing in a soft clench,
Dreaming your wiry house –
Poor toy, my little pet,
So still and listening –

Is it a failing echo,
The lament of the genus,
That calls to this dim corner
So far from Syria?

The Return

Returning from an arid land
(All night her olive groves
Had stirred under the *suspiro de Moro*)
I saw the evening lay a blue-grey arm,
Embankment to embankment, on the Thames.
Half-traced, the colour of the sky,
My image in the window of the train,
A grave transparency.
                                        Victoria:
A village with a station –
Gate of the city, where I was set down
Among the lost commuters of the world:
I tried to speak but found no dialect,
Hearing a cry that shook the continent.
And London sighed to far Andalusia –
Across her mountains and the shouting seas –
As if no other language could express
The fear in the blood of the people,
The agony of the waters,
Of roots that suffer in the grieving earth.

The Bed

Waking to sallow light,
I shift position in
the comfortable hard
bed I have made in my
unrestful sleep a place
of tangled warmth that still
feels dampish where the sheet
exposes hand and arm.

All night my body tried
to mend its blood and wept
a lamina of sweat
through its integument –
that once so live it burned
to hold and gratify
the naked strength it sought –
to tear itself apart.

The Scaffolders

Before I fall awake,
　　they have begun to raise
one level of the structure that will take
　　　　a full two days
　　　　to make complete
round three sides of the house across the street.

　　Hot, naked to the waist,
　　one of athletic build
stands half way as the hollow rods are placed:
　　　　he is so skilled –
　　　　his almost-dance
a part of action, risk, the love of chance.

　　Intrepid acrobats –
　　becoming, as they climb
into their element, agile as cats.
　　　　Taking his time,
　　　　one gets so high,
he whistles as his shoulders brush the sky.

At the Lake

No god has made him but the sun
Has rolled invisible leaves of fire
Across his shoulder blades and down
His lean long body. Round his feet,
The lake is slung in glinting lines,
Bound for the shadows of his hands.

Lac de Castelgaillard, France

All Day the Rain

All day the rain
Drags at the light of things. Especially
At these: the burned-out flares,
Shot from the wound in the heart of genius,
To flash, minutely red, disconsolate,
And die in the cornea.
                              Everywhere,
Always in silence, always
Without effect, knowing he will fall down,
Man weeps to man,
And is afraid of rain. – Or because the sky
Harbours indifference, shaking its cloud
In a black fist, over a scrawl of trees.
– He is ashamed because the leaves keep falling –
Always in silence, always
Finding himself alone in the same street,
That has no birds.
                              All day the rain
Drags at the light of things.

September Journey

Eastbound, under a crag-dark sky –
Bouldering clouds
Have massed over the train, its girdered wheels
Ground shudderingly still,
Between London and the sea. Down on the bank,
Wet flowers of autumn weed
Glow by the track. Dense intercoiling stems
Explore the alien steel, testing a sleeper,
Or scrabble their tendrils in the loose chipped stone –
Seeming, as they encroach,
To multiply.
               Is it this live machine –
The slung reticulated wires,
Its wheels like trellises –
They touch for? Do they sense
A keener radiance – the warmth of skin?
What if the trees –
Dartled with yellow fire –
Lean down dark garages of leaves,
Locking their crankled roots across the rails?

The soil has judged us.
               Then ask forgiveness:
For the burning of the forest,
For the murder of the creatures,
And the poison in the river,
And of the rain, that hangs
In bouldering clouds, under the crag-dark sky.

The Turning Circus

for Jenny MacKilligin

Drunk in the afternoon,
I sip the expensive wine
In a bar off Hanover Square,
Next to a kangaroo vine
And three men talking money
Over continental lager.

Convinced that he is funny –
Recounting a late lost bet
On the age of a colleague –
One loosens his collar to let
The heat of his fervour escape him
As he starts the story over.

These three belong here completely –
Deaf, in their rising elation,
To the song in the wind at the window;
The lament of a generation
For whom the city was furnished
With infinite promise of fortune.

Hard cash is cold currency; yet
We inhabit a state to be cherished –
In our separate worlds we can savour
The tang of an over-priced claret,
Or continental lager,
Reassured that, at least, we *deserve* it

And we never need talk to each other,
And there'll always be someone to blame.
And perhaps I will sit here for ever,
For the night is a turning circus,
And the wind outside will never
Let us forget our shame.

But, dear, I am coming to meet you,
Inside the appointed doorway.
We'll ride in a glittering taxi
Around the turning circus,
And always talk to each other.
And the wind shall repeat our story.

Early November

The day was gold early and I went out under the wind
Over the vivid leaves as they were singing in whispers –
A high day with a blue brim riding the roof-backs,
Leaving the trees red in amazement at their own brightness.
Down Piccadilly to the Circus on a sleek fourteen,
I went, in my long coat, into the heart of town,
Alighted, danced with several people, kissed one I knew
Whose cheek was blushed with cold, called at a bar in Poland Street,
And overheard the discourse of a dozen thirsty souls.

The day was old early and I went back in sudden rain
Under lamps, by windows flushed with light in upper rooms,
Among people dancing out of offices and stores
Into the brilliant streets and the cool ballroom of evening,
Over the dark-drowned leaves that were singing in whispers.

Sleep, Spirit, in your Branching Bed

Sleep, spirit, in your branching bed,
Lie down under the lawns and spread
A frost over your fallen dead.
The hands of stars meet overhead –
Sleep, spirit, in your branching bed.

The Field

Above the once industrial town,
Where necessary buildings stand –
Brick houses in the eighties' style,
The same but for diversely painted doors –
There used to be a field,
A graveyard and a ruined church;
Lilac and blackthorn, jungles of meadow-sweet.

Close to my mother's house,
And far enough away
From the dark mansion where I went to school,
This was my universe.

Among the long-untended graves
Of Watsons, Jacksons, Cleggs –
Narcissus and wild daffodils,
Useful on birthdays (more exotic gifts
Came from our neighbour's garden) and below,
Luminous ranks of rose-bay willow-herb:
Food for the hawk-moth larva; in September,
A drift of seeds.
                                One special friend
Was welcome there – a big rough girl
Called Alison, who fought
Most of my battles. An average gang of boys,
Discouraged by her size and wrestler's gait,
Would never have believed
Her gentle ways with animals or flowers.

The new estates pile up against these hills,
Their regular gardens fenced and cleared of trees.
In small car parks,
Children are playing electronic games.
I want to tell them certain miracles.

In the Garden

I

Dream-deep and heavy
The swing of my waking –
Night had rocked me under,
Safe in her oubliette.

I come back slowly,
Out of a broken landscape
And a deserted dwelling.
This was my mother's garden –
Its blue gate on a string,
And the mock-orange tree
Weighted with halves of bricks.
Strange detail.
                    But already,
What brought me to this place
Relinquishes, draws back –
Blurring all context.
                              It is
As if I had not dreamed
But seen: for an instant only,
To have been real there.

I lift the gate, falling
Forward into daylight.

II

This ground is difficult.
Old walls are buried here.
I have a spoon, a rusted nail
And my two hands.
                              I am planting
Nasturtium seeds – when they have grown
I can eat them. The best part
Is the sweet spur behind
The flower.
                    Digging is fun –
                                        the smell of soil.

This is my patch of ground, between the gate
And the mock-orange tree.
Here I shall plant whatever I can find –
Something with sturdy roots
That comes up every year.

I found a lump of marble in the yard –
It might be useful.
                              If I build
A miniature landscape, this rock
Could be a mountain.
                              I had better clear
Space for a forest with my little spoon.

III

Darkness commend them to a track of leaves
Who love their shape. Let the dark forms impose
A tense half-fallen stillness, where the blood races
Through wings of lovers in the veils of grass.

Tonight, in this cool place by a velvet river,
Hands meet in the sound of the amen of water –
Here, where breathless woods return the whisper
Of heart to fiery heart through the dense cover.

Walk with me to the gate of a quiet garden,
Where scents of invisible flowers compound and deepen –
Holding each other, finding the gate open,
While people among the shadows rise and beckon.

Under the leaves, by this cool watershed,
Alone together we shall make our bed.

IV

O brothers, sisters –
Look how the garden fills
With too much light,
And how the rain
Burns in the crown
Of the mock-orange tree.

Beyond the gate,
The garden of the world –
Observe the extent
And impact of our works:
The ocean rises
At the delta.

That sound, that sound
Is the screaming
In the forest –
The rending of timber
And the dispossession
Of the creatures.

In the cold hills
Above the city
A child leans on his gun.
Elsewhere, he starves to death
And has no burial
In the dry ground.

Murder and rape
Are the inheritors.
We have no language
And nothing is audible
But the machinery
Of vengeance.

O brothers, sisters –
Look how the grass withers,
How the stream vanishes –
Look how the rain
Burns in the crown
Of the mock-orange tree.

Island Visit

for David Gascoyne

Drank a gin coming down –
Fast out of Waterloo.
Mainland gusty in blondshine,
Then, light-bound on Solent water,
Bladed with sun, my boat bumps at the harbour.
I see you in front of the sky, with Judy, waving.

Later, in the glare
Of your front living room
After a simple lunch,
You show me some of the books
You could not live without – Pierre Jean Jouve –
Treasure from Parton Street or the Rue de l'Odéon.

Discomfited somehow,
You return to your favourite chair,
Who was in love in Paris –
That night in '38
At Place Dauphine under the chestnut trees,
Alone in silence with your *jeune Danois*.

You help me to a drink,
But tell me you must wait
Till seven-thirty sharp –
Relying as you do
On the routine you need to keep you sane,
Having fallen on that *chemin des abîmes*

That led you through the wastes
Of tortuous middle age
And broke you more than once,
Though you survive it seems,
Safe on your island. Tomorrow I return
To a world where you were never at your ease.

You read from Marianne Moore
And seem to take such strength
From images that ring
Like pæans from your lips.
You listen to my poems. As I look up,
A kindling flame disturbs your level gaze.

Hammersmith, Excuse Me

for my mother

'*Dance in the old-fashioned way,*' croons Aznavour,
From two colossal speakers in mid-air.
Unwanted chaperon, I fetch the tea
In polystyrene cups. As I return

The Latin King is holding out his hand –
An invitation to a lilting rumba.
You smile acceptance and with *Spanish Eyes,*
Go turning in your starry element.

You're up for every number – *California Blue,*
The Breeze and I and *Lady is a Tramp.*
I sit among the ranks of single men,
Moved by your art – the energy and grace

Inherent in each step, practised for years
At Blackpool Tower; in grand Mancunian halls.
An average floor, you say: but I'm impressed,
As you disco with a man who's twice your size

(It's *Boogie Woogie Bugle Boy* this time) –
And wonder if the kids on Friday night
Feel half your joy in living, are aware
That one quick step is often all it takes.

Going North

for *Michael Schmidt*

Half an hour from Euston and already
The sun, it seems, has travelled far enough,
Preferring the mutable palette of the Thames –
Artful with rooftops and the sides of towers,
Slick in the City, idle in Green Park.
It's odd and a bit depressing, this going North –
Though it's where I started – when I had my health,
And didn't smoke, drank mainly at weekends,
And slept with my first boy.
                              In Stalybridge –
My mother's town, half urban, half serene
With factory woods and desolate canals –
A paradise of walks and *nice old pubs*,
Newt-fishing and the yammering of birds –
And, how could I forget, that bloody school.

It can't be far now. Something about the light
Alters perception of the falling land –
A sense of urgency, of losing time,
As though I'd come without some vital key.
At Crewe the sky turns uniformly grey,
And who can blame it. Further up the line
Old Manchester sits in the cold and waits for rain.

It's not a cultural desert I remember
(Though I probably missed a trick or two in my teens)
Or why would you have struck such sturdy roots?
It's good to know you're up here running things,
That we'll have lunch and gossip in *The Italia*.
And yet it never feels like coming home,
Wherever that may be. Perhaps it's where
The heart lies, like a room in Kensington,
In Mexico. The Cheshire fields fly south.
At Jodrell Bank they're talking to the stars.

Edvard Munch

The shadow of the window on the floor –
A double cross cast by the moon,
Night in St Cloud – lengthens from where he sits,
Your friend, the poet, indistinct except
For sinister top hat
And one arm propped against the window pane.
But now it's you –
Painter of the agonising stillness
In the death chamber –
Mourning your sister by the dark river,
In a Paris suburb far from Christiania.

Another room: a frail pubescent girl –
Her shadow on the wall behind,
A huge black phallus, looms above the bed.
Horror contracts her shoulders and these eyes –
Mirrors of inexperience that stare
Into the staring faces of the crowd –
That *Evening on Karl Johan* – or, confused,
Follow the dance at Åsgårdstrand,
Where a smiling woman
Lifts up her lovely hand, impossibly,
Towards love's flower. Her counterpart, in black –
Excluded, motionless –
Looks on in anguish as the moon presides.
– Again it's you –
Painter of the rejection on the shore,
Of kisses that destroy,
Who heard, at sunset, from the dark blue hills,
An endless scream filling the sky with blood.

A vampiress, a sensual Madonna,
Love bears her ashes to your grave.
Cold in your fist, a broken heart –
Your vision of eternity, its flower.

Poem on St Patrick's Day

Woke on St Patrick's Day
From a dream of my own death
Wracked in an old man's body
Under a heavy sheet,
And caught my breath
And lifted off the quilt.

I looked and found you sleeping,
And could not find a name
For what turned in an instant
From waking fear –
Relief? No, not relief.
You are more to me than that.

Half Irish, you
Will celebrate this day
With shamrock in your coat,
Drink after work
And telephone abroad,
Your mother's eldest son.

I lose weight and our bed's
Less comfortable these days.
So, while I can get out,
I'll go down in the light
Of a new season,
To where you are dancing.

The Playground Bell

Dead drunk by nine – this used to be enough.
In Manchester I went out every night;
Picked up and stayed wherever there was drink
With men whose names were last thing on my mind –
Including one who slung the Union Jack
Over his bedside lamp for atmosphere,
On the Last Night of The Proms in eighty-two;
My first 'experience': even the white socks
I'd been advised to wear were a success –
One foot displayed, half-casually, to mark
My absolute virginity. The final touch:
My mother fixed a blow-wave in my hair.

Always indulgent towards her only son
(Lucky for me my parents got divorced),
She must have sensed I wasn't the same boy
Who'd walked for twenty miles or more a day
On gritstone tracks, over the backs of hills –
The Pennine wastes of Bleaklow, Kinder Scout.

The landscape of the city was more harsh:
Bleaker than any tract of mountain peat,
The bus ride down the Manchester Old Road.
In Sackville Street, between the Thomson's Arms
And the Rembrandt Hotel, a universe
Peopled by drunks and rent boys – one a punk,
Who used to leave his girlfriend at the bar
On business. After barely half an hour,
He'd stroll back in and stand them both a drink.

I quickly learned the language and the code –
Had 'sisters' who were kind men twice my age,
Who paid for beers and thought I was mature;
Confided, gave advice and lent me fares.
On Saturday nights we'd drive to Liverpool
Or Stoke-on-Trent, as if there were a difference
Between one seedy night-spot and another –
Though local accents used to turn me on,
And that rare prize – a genuine foreigner
On holiday, was worth the taxi ride
To some remote hotel. Leaving in secret,
Before breakfast, pocketing an address
(In Paris!) I would never write to, a poignant act.

One Christmas I saved up and went to Heaven –
The biggest dive in England, under Charing Cross –
A three-tiered circuit ranged by packs of men,
And boys who came to dance. I ended up
In a basement somewhere off the Chepstow Road,
And woke to the first snow-fall of the year.
I came to London for a long weekend
And stayed; met someone famous who was kind,
And took a boring job in Portland Place.
I went, on summer nights, to Hampstead Heath,
Where pints of beer at Jack Straw's Castle gave
To sex under the tents of holly trees –
Shadows of hands that flowered through the dusk:
No names, no contracts, but each parting hug
Was less a token of civility
Than an act of love.
                    Later, in Amsterdam,
In crowded cellars on the Warmoesstraat,
The rules were different – a more serious art,
Practised in uniform. The smell of leather
An aphrodisiac keen as the scent of leaves;
And still, the magic of indifference.

It still goes on – wherever hands can find
Response of hands; hold, in the hollow silence,
A tangible warmth, the heartbeat in the dark
Where death has entered, ringing the playground bell.
It hurts the ear. It echoes through the woods.

I stare at death in a mirror behind the bar
And wonder when I sacrificed my blood,
And how I could not recognise the face
That smiled with the mouth, the eyes, of death –
In Manchester, London or Amsterdam.
I do not hate that face, only the bell.